With These Wings

Blessings, A. Shea

www.linktr.ee/a.shea

a collection of poetry and prose by
Angie Shea

Angie Shea
Georgia, USA
asheawaters.com

WITH THESE WINGS/Angie Shea 1ˢᵗ Edition
ISBN 978-1-7372810-9-2

Angie Shea

Foreword

Chances are you have purchased this book because you have connected with Angie Shea's ability to identify with your innermost feelings. How many times have you stumbled across her words on social media and been struck by the way they mirror your own thoughts? She bravely uses her voice for the silent sufferers who cling to her words as their inspirational ladder. Her metaphorical style breathes with confessions and levitates the hearts of warriors.

Angie Shea is not only a talented writer. She is also an accomplished artist. Her hand painted work graces the interior and covers of countless modern day poetry books. Now, in her solo poetry debut "With These Wings", she combines creative visual art along with her unique poetry imagery. This book is so much more than heartfelt poetry. It is truly the heart of a poet.

It is my hope that this exceptional work of art touches you as much as it has me.

Always a fan,

Alfa Holden
Author of bestselling books I Find You in the Darkness, She Wears Pain Like Diamonds, and 6 other poetry books.

Angie Shea

To my sons...

my wings.

Angie Shea

With wings broken
  and brushing the ground
   or etching ether above the clouds,
I can never regret the flight of my heart
           The aftermath is always art

A pale beauty
that hides the scars
painted so well
in your words of art,
untouched, but broken,
shattered, yet so very whole,
an enigma
that raises not questions
but the banners of hope

You think the calm defines her,
that she is all fragility and grace…
but this quiet one is lion-hearted,
and when that ferocity wakes,
she is a **warrior**
with not a drop of surrender
in her veins

Life is falling
through layers of fire and water,
burnt beyond recognition
and baptized anew,
over and over
until we become ruins
of our own beautiful truth

We say the stars are in repose,
but what if there are those
in rebellious respite
taking their place
far and away,
untamed light that escapes
to stretch its wings
to a quiet place
where a heart can scream

We are a dying breed –
the warriors
with hope filled eyes
and bleeding hearts
who beat their chests
and scream their lover's name
in a war cry…

the ones who never let love
go down without a fight

Sometimes hope
is the rope
you must let go of
to experience the fall
   and the revealing crawl
   back to what you deserve

Heaven knows
this life is languid,
but it is mine

No feeble flesh
will steal away
my heart's desire
to shine

With beautiful words,
she unearths
her deepest wounds
and darkest loves

I'm going to walk right out
of this heavy heart
into the bare boned beauty
of a new start

And if I am a disaster,
I am the one that will blow you away
with what beauty can be born
from storms

These wings grow heavier
the more I fight for the sky,
but still I stand a little taller
after every try

*The way her heart rolls out like thunder
and crashes for those she loves…*

> that is a courage
> we need more of

I feel it coming...
the wind of change,
the overturning leaf,
a smell of freedom in the air,
a rush of fresh belief

No more shame on my face
No more doubt in my voice

There is a storm coming
yet again,
but this time
it is a choice

She is walking away
afraid,
but brave
White knuckles
become open arms
Now, she is ready
to embrace the stars

I am a million shattered pieces
of the girl I used to be,
and not all will survive this mending
Some are obsolete
I am scarred,
but I am bending
so not to break with every beat
of this fragile, bleeding heart
I have conquered hell to keep

Show me who you are
when it's **dark**
   It is never the light
   that reveals the truth

Search the darkness closely
When the monsters come out,
so do the heroes

Scars dot the dark spaces
in her mind
like constellations
in a chalkboard sky,
each a story
she fights to rewrite
into a victory

I pour it out,
so my sanity is saved
  because I must
  make something beautiful
  from all this pain

You are beautifully undone,
torn apart so young
that the hell still lines your veins
But, it's that burn
that keeps your heart awake

These days, she is falling
more than she flies,
losing more
than she has found
But, she refuses to waste a day
with her wings on the ground

What the darkness grows,
it does not own
Emerge from the shadows with a glow
so strong
the angels turn their face,
so ruthless
the demons fear your name

I want to feel like the moon
as it takes the sky –
  bright with the confidence
  of my own rise
  in any darkness

I am my ancestor's strength –
forests of sadness
burnt away
only to drown
in a landslide
of bittersweet pain
and spark my heart
against the rock
that tried to claim me

She arose from that pain
like a rose after rain
   smelling of hope
   and fresh dreams

I care less and less
what others think
and more and more
about becoming
the woman my heart
has the courage to be

The poetic polarity of life:
agony and bliss
fragility and strength

and hearts that live both sides,
growing the most beautiful wings

I am courage with thin skin,
a beast with a pretty face
Never underestimate the meek ones…
savage hearts with a touch of grace

This wound may have me
on my knees,
but while I am kneeling,
I will bloom where I bleed

The battles often plague my mind,
but my heart is still in the fight,
and that is the only way
to win a war

Some hearts are suns
in graying skies
that rise
to warm the world

Let me walk with you
while you are bleeding
I will hold your hand
while you roam
I know the unmapped spaces
of a broken heart
are too dark
to confront alone

I never recognized myself,
never spied the beauty
of my own soul
until I stopped trying to see "me"
in mirrors others chose

Just a flesh and blood girl
  tender heart
  thin skin
that this monstrous world
sunk its teeth in
and bred a **w a r r i o r**

Be a flower
in the concrete cold,
a beacon bloom
with colors that glow
amidst the hate,
iron mettle
beneath satin petals
no darkness can taint

Every blow that shattered me,
created me
Color in every shard
from that glass and metal
I put a girl together
with lead lined scars
I forged my stained-glass heart,
and when the light gets in
I am even more beautiful

I feel it grow
as the past lets go…
that flame
at the base of my heart
burning away the leather
that has held it together,
unveiling a warmth
that thins the scars
just like oblivion
creates the stars

Still there are moments
where I see stars,
where I go blind
with a rush of hope
that later fades into
the bits of gold
always dancing
in my eyes

You thought you could snuff me out
with your poison tongue and violence,
but here I am,
rising up
in this new beauty and defiance

The world
has stained
my mind
with chaos
and darkness,
but my heart
is divine...
too brilliant
to tarnish

Anyone can admire the flowers
Give me the ones who praise the roots
and the strength beneath the blooms

Ashes turn to gold…
the kind you cannot hold
or spend,
the priceless kind
that mends the cracks
and keeps your softness in

Not all that is strong
is impenetrable and cold
Warm flesh
and an open heart...
the mettle of true armor

Silver linings girl
with a heart of gold,
braver than your mind
though it beats with pain,
that gilded weight
has an unbreakable shine

Bitterness
is a weakness
diluting
the sweetness
that flows through life
in trickles or waves

and we each decide
which one to taste

There is road rash on my soul
from the ways I have been thrown away
Scars – years of friendship wide –
and family gifted knives
that stay
underneath my skin,
pressed against rib and spine,
so many ways, torn apart
and still
the hope in my heart
survives

Live full every day…
the flowers that grow
in the soil of your soul
are meant to adorn your life
not your grave

The weight of the world
often lands on broken shoulders,
but that deeper wound
becomes the root
of the strongest wings

Yes...I am a survivor,
and with every breath I will be,
but it is as a fighter
I pray you remember me,
not for my life's struggles,
but for the way I gave them beauty

It is both a blessing and a curse
that I am forever soft
beneath this armor

I am a hero in a puddle
on the ground
This human heart
weighs me down
Some days I can't find my feet,
much less the sky
There is no super power
in this blood,
just an inborn will to fight
I keep a tourniquet in my pocket
to give my heart some time to cry
Is that still admiration in your eyes?

Quiet
in my fear of words...
they echo and are rarely heard
Screams are silenced
as *"life is tough,"*
and being the strongest
is not strong enough
when we still break

Sometimes, I wonder
how much stronger
I can take

I will not pour it out slowly
My heart overflows
It can no longer be contained
It swells like a river,
dammed to be tamed
Now. I invite the flood

Her heart is rekindled
You can see the flame in her eyes
Hellfire backfired
Now she's more than alive

I am in awe of the stars
(tiny beacons in a black abyss)
I long to be that kind of soul

We praise silence
as if it is strength,
mock tears
as if they are weak
when vulnerable is beautiful,
and it's the **bravest**
who bare their feelings

Before the world stepped in
and defined your worth,
before your value hinged
on being tough,
you were the softest thing
this side of heaven…
and you were beautiful

They don't own me:
  the demons,
  the dark seas,
  the scars,
  the disease
They are just bullies
that my heart beats
every single day

Grab life by the minute,
and chase hope
wherever you can get it
Squeeze the joy
from every second
of your life
We are heaven
in mortal clothes,
and every beat
of these hearts know
that we are created
to do more
than just survive

The strongest warriors
are armed
with something
To believe in

I am alive
in the midnights and dawns
of a fervent soul
that is filled with eons,
like a thimble
trying to contain the sea

I feel the years in my bones...
the aged wisdom of my soul,
but my spirit has a youth
that time and pain
will never touch

We are not these stale eyes
and shriveled lungs
defining our spirits by years
We are embers of youth
that continuously burn
beneath the weight
of aging fears

There are days,
floating away…
tethered to nothing
but a fraying dream,
that I am reminded
of the years I survived
holding on
with just a heartstring

The wishful sight
of this rose-colored heart,
even in shards…
it's not the cracks
that catch my eye
but the beauty
that rushes to fill them

Some souls travel
long, lonely roads
of valley and shadow
to see their first light
And often,
on the way,
they become it

Every time you break me,
I will mend
Each time you bury me,
I will rise
Throw everything you've got
at my warrior heart,
and watch me
do more than survive

I am grateful
and unashamed
to house a heart
that was razed
over and again
and still
blooming brave

Angie Shea

I write in tears
and daydreams,
sweet songs
and steep screams,
through bloodshot nights
and rose-tinted dawns

I am every one of these,
and I own them all

Strong hearts
are not made of metal,
but of darkness, tears, and failure
that taught them the power
of even the softest light

Light is burning
through this veil
of blackened tears
and heavy sighs,
brightening the air
with resounding hellos,
dissolving the echoes
of cold goodbyes

The whole of my heart is weary,
but my adrenaline soul
raises me to hope,
and I fight for every drop
of this life

We need to stop
promoting silence
as some kind of strength,
and people who feel
everything deeply
should never be defined as weak

I am clay still being thrown
by a wheel
not done with me,
still rough around the edges
and oh so tender in-between,
picking up the gold
as I grow and bleed,
the evolving form
of the fearless woman
I am ever striving to be

Trying to go with the flow,
but these bruises show
it's more like tumbling
Such unforgiving terrain
and the currents of pain
are swift and humbling
So many years, walking blind,
staying the course in my mind
though the view was crumbling
Believing as long as my heart
was my loving north star,
these footfalls were not stumbling
but steadily leading me home

I am grateful
for losing my way
Having no path
forced me to forge one,
and I became more myself
with every step

Even on the grueling days
when reality bites too hard,
I may hang my head for a little while,
but my eyes are still full of stars

There are silver lines
in every struggle,
diamond dust
in the saddest eyes,
golden hearts
beneath love-poor shoulders,
bits of hope
with priceless shine...

the treasures
we must fight to find

I wear it proud,
my wildflower crown,
no jewels or
family crests
Fashioned with blooms
from every wound,
I am a queen
who rules herself

Some days,
hope feels like a war,
and feeling at all
is brave
But I have seen giving up
It's not peace...
it's a grave

There is a refuge in paper
I find nowhere else...
blank canvas awaiting purpose
from the depths of myself
to soak up the river
that flows from my heart
and turns that pain
into a pouring
that is poetry or art

Yes, the sadness will sway
the ocean in your eyes,
but who says you can't move
mountains when you cry?

They will lift their heads
as you fly higher,
either with smiles
proud and inspired
or holding their breath
for your decline,
and that is the telling
of who belongs in your life

Let it ache
Let it bleed
Let it take you
to your knees
in sweetest rapture,
but please
my ferocious heart
never settle

...and I have died
a little inside,
lost bits of hope
along the way,
when despite my love
and sincerity,
I am broken and betrayed,
but then a stranger
plants a seed,
becomes a flower
that is a friend,
and my heart
learns that a loss
does not have to be an end

I was never
rainbows and butterflies
(born into a life
of cloudy, death grip days)
but I became Phoenix fire
and silver linings...
all the things that saved me

Courage is the beacon light
of an embattled heart
that is itself in need of hope
but still shines

I was always too full of something...
too much sight to follow blindly,
too much conscience for lying down,
too many words,
too many emotions
and not enough voices
telling me it is all beautiful

Angie Shea

My heart is a morning star –
a light refusing to fade
a power defying the dark

I am not sorry
anymore
for breaking bars
and cutting cords
I will not fit in
So. love me as I am

My broken was not beautiful
It was raging despair and decay
Emaciated by darkness,
I would have wasted away,
but for that aching sparkle
like gold dust inside my bones,
a marrow cloaked rebellion,
a river of molten hope

Never let the scars
become the softest parts
of your heart

These days of darkness will fade,
and love will find me
looking down on this valley,
standing in the light
of my whole heart

Even the stars have scars,
a darkness
in the depth of their light
But what we see
is a beauty
whole and bright
because those holes
(like yours and mine)
are on the inside

Finally,
I realized
these dreams
need no one's belief
but mine

It stormed yesterday
Pieces of me
were swept away,
But, this time I did not mourn
In their release,
a strength was born,
a certainty in my soul
that what was to come
would always be greater
than what needed to be let go

Memories and wounds –
like a burial shroud,
like a gravity
that weighs my spirit down,
that try to hold me
to this unfertile ground…
but I go on fighting
to kiss the clouds

Hope has withered
The flames have died,
but within the embers,
the best of you survived

Against the wind,
despite the cards,
I am here...
all wings and hearts.

In the face of violence,
she bloomed,
all tender petals
and titanium roots,
an unwitting rebel
in unspoken truth,
an anthem
even in her silence

Ineffable strength
in those bits
of steel and string
become her wings

Now I am comfortable
in this skin...
it fits the size of my heart

I am a sea of untamed things,
kept quiet and deep
beneath years of storms
and sunken dreams,
now fighting for the surface

There is a melody behind the beats
of my much-too-human heart
In love or in pain,
I can never find the pause
In sheer rebellion,
some days,
it plays on and on...
ever loving,
ever hoping
to live a beautiful song

Let it go!
Grab hold of what comes next
with white knuckles and gratitude
Fly forward...
away from the past,
and burn bright
in every moment you still have

Fireflies in a jar,
a salt lamp,
a wishing star…
be a light left on
wherever you are
because the darkness
never sleeps

My body may be
compromised with pain,
my mind foggy
with shades of gray,
but there is no darkness
that can dull or sway
the pure fire in my heart

I am reaching for hope
amidst this chaos
of dreams and reality
The past is falling away
and *for once*
I am not focused
on the debris
I am looking up
My eyes have a death grip
on the sky,
and I am not letting go
(come what may)
Every day,
I
will
rise

There is no sickness
in your sadness,
no weakness
in your velvet bones
Some are melancholy souls
always searching for heaven
because they have survived
so much hell alone

Sail on
without the wind,
without a star in the sky,
adrift
on a restless sea...
trusting your own light

Never be small
to avoid being alone
or to maintain a comfort zone
Be that big, beautiful soul
that explores and owns
every inch of your life

An iron will
and backbone of steel
do not require
a hard heart

Born into a sadness
I could not escape,
tempted often
to let the tears suffocate
my burgeoning fire,
but my heart became consumed
with a ravenous desire
to burn free
and be so much more
than what was done to me

My
darkness
is as
honest
as my
fire

I would steal the shine
from a thousand stars,
wrestle the moon
for his place in the sky,
be a single firefly
in your darkness...
  whatever light
  wakes the fight
  in your eyes

Let me live slow,
deep,
in the throes
of a soulful life
and the sweetest love,
so that my heart
feels a lifetime
in these reckoning years
and worries not
for what was

Sometimes
I am frightened of tomorrow,
of the ifs and the buts,
of the shadow of this sorrow,
of still being too much
Yet I can cede to nothing,
knowing no other way
than to start each morning
being proud of yesterday
and the miracle
that there is somehow
still fight in me today

I am a shell
of what I had dreamed,
cracked and,
in some ways,
incomplete,
but the reality
of that "blissful" me
was like reaching the moon
with no stops between
So, I have been
a hundred different stars
in this sky of life,
sometimes empty,
forever scarred,
but my heart
was always a light,
always burning,
and maybe that
is my perfect

Dreams I thought
had died,
been pushed aside,
mutilated to fit
an average life
are now revived,
and I
am saved

She was brave
in the face of pain,
the way a palm
soaks in the rain
but still stands strong
against the winds
Her heart breaks,
but her spine only bends

I want to live every line of this story,
the chapters bleeding into each other
Though years grow shorter,
the sweetest moments lengthen every day,
and the pain becomes only a page

Time to pick up these ashes
and start walking
The mountains are calling,
and the life I deserve
is on the other side

Angie Shea

Kindness floats,
and I breathe lighter
with those bits of hope
in my lungs

What a beautiful breeze
in this desert of stony hearts
If there were more like you,
they could hold the stars
because you burn,
forgetting the weather,
your softest parts
keeping it all together...
you are the wind of change

The bits of dreams
left scattered
along the highway
of my regret
were like a trail
my heart followed
back to myself

I have lived many lives
in the space of one
I don't recognize some of my faces,
but I celebrate the beauty
I have become

We are not long upon
this whirling dirt,
so let us plant our feet
like seeds
of hopeful words
and grow into stories
that save the earth

I lost many years in a cage
(a chained soul and a
tied tongue to match)
Now freedom flows
like liquid flight in my veins,
and I soar honestly,
on my own
Met with love or hate,
I will not hold back
I will not go back
to that prison

These are the kind of tides
that never mind the moon,
but the ebb and flow
of boiling blood
as it rushes through
a heart fighting for light

Another sunrise
met with wide eyes
that take each ray of gold
into these bankrupt veins
and spin it into hope

...if we only held on
to life every day
like we do
when we are afraid
of losing it

Dance with sorrow
when it is your partner,
when you cannot keep time
with hope
Step into the arms
of what your heart
is facing,
and embrace it
until it lets go

The deaths I have died
will never outweigh
the bits of life
I garnered and gave
in return

There are things that cannot die
when all else is burned away,
alive in the ash and decay,
a remnant of life
like a star in the frigid dark
When all seems lost,
you will find the warmth
from the flame
of your own heart

Sadness rolls over me
with the weight of an angry sea,
and still my heart refuses to beat
to the tune of a eulogy
It is a love song
all my own
that daily rescues me

I have been too long
on the ground,
buried
or face down,
aching for the sky
Now, the wind
has found my wings,
and with every strength
of my being,
I swear
I will fly.

What a beautiful weakness
to feel so much
My sensitivity
is always brought up
as a flaw,
but I will never change
the range,
the depth of feeling
that kept me awake,
the tenderness
that made me this strong

I am brave
in my own way...

I am ferociously soft

What they tried to put down,
tried to stomp into the ground
to feel taller,
to make you feel smaller
because their own hearts
already were…
is a brilliance that now
they fight to ignore

My heart is rooted in kindness
Your mud might stain my skin,
but I grew up deep…
a red clay goddess
that ugliness
will never sink in

This lesson was a breakthrough
to the other side of me,
to the Wonderland of my own strength,
to the Eden of loving me

You think the end is beneath
Trust your heart again
f r e e f a l l
It was just a moment you could not
feel your wings

I will walk gracefully
through these miles of life
Running
has bruised my feet,
and I missed parts of "me"
while merely glancing at scenery
that passes only once
Now my toes grip the earth
in fierce defiance,
and I take in
every nuance

You think no one else understands
the depth of your sad song
until you open the window to let it out
and a thousand voices sing along

Within the frame
of these delicate wings
exists the most
unbreakable of things

I have grown tired
of the past haunting me
and all the weight
that it brings
Time to bleed dead stories
from my veins
and erase these names
from my wings

My hope is often written
on the wings
of what is to come,
and every kindness
is a feather
adding strength
to carry on

So far away
from where I thought
I would be,
but closer to the girl
who wholly believed
in her dreams
and the woman
who will fight for them

I feel it on the edge
of every footstep.
The wind is shifting
to my back
The fight is turning
to flight,
and I can almost
taste the sky

I go to war
every day
for my loves,
for my life
My warrior heart
floods these veins
with unyielding light

**Giving up
is truly not
in my blood**

Angie Shea

Acknowledgements

I would like to thank my son Patrick for being my reason and loving me "as is" always. You are amazing. Never forget that. I love you Beanie.

This book would still be in procrastination mode if not for the continuous support of my editor/designer and one of my best friends Ashley Jane. Her gentle pushing and aggressive reminders of my work's value made this possible. Her skills and friendship amaze me daily.

As she is to many, Alfa Holden is a huge inspiration in my writing and pursuit of publishing. I am beyond honored to have her write the foreword for this book. We are a part of each other's daily support system, and I am blessed to call her friend. Thank you for believing in me Alfa. I adore you.

Gypsy Mercer has been a loyal friend and support in both my professional and personal life. Thank you for your presence and love without reservation my talented friend.

Alissa, you are an amazing woman and a warrior style friend like I have never known. Thank you for the generous wind beneath my wings that you are always so willing to provide and for reminding me of who I am and all I can accomplish by just being me. I love you.

Wesley, thank you for always supporting me and believing in me.

To all the members of the online writing communities who gave me advice, encouragement, and support, I appreciate you. To all my readers and followers on all platforms, thank you for getting me to this moment. My heart is full of gratitude.

About the Author

Angie Shea (A. Shea) is an Indie writer and artist from Georgia. She attended Auburn University and holds a master's degree in psychology from Liberty University. The mother of two grown boys, Angie is now focusing on pursuing her dream of writing and art.

Poetry has been a part of her life since early childhood when she first began writing. An avid reader in her teens, classic literature and poets stole her heart. The inspiration for her own work comes from her struggles with chronic illness and past trauma and the importance of not only surviving but soaring.

When not working on her writing or art, Angie enjoys the outdoors, art museums, travel, reading and relaxing with her dogs. One of her favorite mottos is from Friedrich Nietzsche, "Those who have a 'why' to live, can bear with almost any 'how'."

You can find more from Angie at:

Poetry
Facebook: www.facebook.com/a.sheawriter
Instagram: @a.shea_writer

Art
Facebook: www.facebook.com/ashea.artistry
Instagram: @ashea.artistry

www.asheawaters.com

61600424R00097